BASEBALL LEGENDS

Hank Aaron
Grover Cleveland Alexander
Ernie Banks
Johnny Bench
Yogi Berra
Roy Campanella
Roberto Clemente
Ty Cobb
Dizzy Dean
Joe DiMaggio
Bob Feller
Jimmie Foxx
Lou Gehrig
Bob Gibson
Rogers Hornsby
Reggie Jackson
Walter Johnson
Sandy Koufax
Mickey Mantle
Christy Mathewson
Willie Mays
Stan Musial
Satchel Paige
Brooks Robinson
Frank Robinson
Jackie Robinson
Babe Ruth
Tom Seaver
Duke Snider
Willie Stargell
Honus Wagner
Ted Williams
Carl Yastrzemski
Cy Young

BASEBALL LEGENDS

WILLIE STARGELL

Mike Shannon

Introduction by
Jim Murray

Senior Consultant
Earl Weaver

CHELSEA HOUSE PUBLISHERS

New York • Philadelphia

Published by arrangement with
Chelsea House Publishers.
Newfield Publications is a federally
registered trademark of Newfield
Publications, Inc.

Produced by James Charlton Associates
New York, New York.

Designed by Hudson Studio
Ossining, New York.

Typesetting by LinoGraphics
New York, New York.

Picture research by Carolann Hawkins
Cover illustration by Dan O'Leary

Library of Congress Cataloging-in-Publication Data

Shannon, Mike.
    Willie Stargell / Mike Shannon ; introduction by Jim Murray ;
senior consultant, Earl Weaver.
        p.   cm. — (Baseball legends)
    Includes bibliographical references (p.) and index.
    Summary: A biography of Willie Stargell, powerful slugger for the
Pittsburgh Pirates.
        ISBN 0-7910-1192-5. — ISBN 0-7910-1226-3 (pbk.)
    1. Stargell, Willie, 1941-   —Juvenile literature.
    2. Baseball players—United States—Biography—Juvenile
literature. 3. Pittsburgh Pirates (Baseball team)—Juvenile literature.
[1. Stargell, Willie, 1941-   . 2. Baseball players.
3. Afro-Americans—Biography.] I. Title. II. Series.
GV865.s76s53 1992   91-16691
796.357'092—dc20   CIP
[B]   AC

CONTENTS

WHAT MAKES A STAR

Jim Murray

No one has ever been able to explain to me the mysterious alchemy that makes one man a .350 hitter and another player, more or less identical in physical makeup, hard put to hit .200. You look at an Al Kaline, who played with the Detroit Tigers from 1953 to 1974. He was pale, stringy, almost poetic-looking. He always seemed to be struggling against a bad case of mononucleosis. But with a bat in his hands, he was King Kong. During his career, he hit 399 home runs, rapped out 3,007 hits, and compiled a .297 batting average.

Form isn't the reason. The first time anybody saw Roberto Clemente step into the batter's box for the Pittsburgh Pirates, the best guess was that Clemente would be back in Double A ball in a week. He had one foot in the bucket and held his bat at an awkward angle—he looked as though he couldn't hit an outside pitch. A lot of other ballplayers may have had a better-looking stance. Yet they never led the National League in hitting in four different years, the way Clemente did.

Not every ballplayer is born with the ability to hit a curveball. Nor is exceptional hand-eye coordination the key to heavy hitting. Big-league locker rooms are filled with players who have all the attributes, save one: discipline. Every baseball man can tell you a story about a pitcher who throws a ball faster than anyone has ever seen but who has no control on or *off* the field.

The Hall of Fame is full of people who transformed themselves into great ballplayers by working at the sport, by studying the game, and making sacrifices. They're overachievers—and winners. If you want to find them, just watch the World Series. Or simply read about New York Yankee great Lou Gehrig; Ted Williams, "the Splendid Splinter" of the Boston Red Sox; or the Dodgers' strikeout king Sandy Koufax.

A pitcher *should* be able to win a lot of ballgames with a 98-miles-per-hour fastball. But what about the pitcher who wins 20 games a year with a fastball so slow that you can catch it with your teeth? Bob Feller of the Cleveland Indians got into the Hall of Fame with a blazing fastball that glowed in the dark. National League star Grover Cleveland Alexander got there with a pitch that took considerably longer to reach the plate; but when it did arrive, the pitch was exactly where Alexander wanted it to be—and the last place the batter expected it to be.

There are probably more players with exceptional ability who didn't make it to the major leagues than there are who did. A number of great hitters, bored with fielding practice, had to be dropped from their team because their home-run production didn't make up for their lapses in the field. And then there are players like Brooks Robinson of the Baltimore Orioles, who made himself into a human vacuum cleaner at third base because he knew that working hard to become an expert fielder would win him a job in the big leagues.

A star is not something that flashes through the sky. That's a comet. Or a meteor. A star is something you can steer ships by. It stays in place and gives off a steady glow; it is fixed, permanent. A star works at being a star.

And that's how you tell a star in baseball. He shows up night after night and takes pride in how brightly he shines. He's Willie Mays running so hard his hat keeps falling off; Ty Cobb sliding to stretch a single into a double; Lou Gehrig, after being fooled in his first two at-bats, belting the next pitch off the light tower because he's taken the time to study the pitcher. Stars never take themselves for granted. That's why they're stars.

1

A SUPER SERIES

Ⅰn the first 75 years of World Series competition, only three teams managed to overcome a three-games-to-one deficit and win the Series. In October 1979, the Pittsburgh Pirates attempted to become the fourth team to accomplish that feat.

The Pirates had shown a lot of poise in winning games 5 and 6 after losing three of the first four games to the Baltimore Orioles. Late-inning rallies in games 5 and 6 had helped Pittsburgh even the Series. Baltimore, however, was an overwhelming favorite to win the seventh and final game. For one thing, the Orioles had history on their side. They also had the advantage of playing game 7 at home.

As it turned out, the Pirates had something even better: first baseman Willie Stargell.

With a baseball bat in his hands, Willie Stargell was truly a menacing sight. For the past 17 years—all in a Pirates uniform—he had ter-

Stargell hits a 3-run homer in the 11th inning of game 1 of the 1979 N.L. championship to give the Pirates a 5–2 victory over the Reds. Cincinnati's Johnny Bench reaches vainly for the pitch by Tom Hume.

rorized National League pitchers with his powerful swing. "I have never seen a batter who hits the ball any harder," former Pirates manager Harry Walker said. "For sheer crack of bat meeting the ball, Stargell simply is the best."

Stargell's trademark warmup when he stepped into the batter's box—twirling the bat in a windmill motion—was enough to make pitchers quake. But he did more than just twirl the bat. He slugged the ball consistently, especially during the 1979 season, when he led the Pirates to victory over the Cincinnati Reds in the National League championship series.

During the first six games of the World Series, Stargell rapped out 8 hits, including 2 home runs and 5 RBIs. But the 38-year-old first baseman was an old man by baseball standards. He was playing on bad knees scarred by several operations. Could the man whom teammates affectionately called Pops lead Pittsburgh to one more victory? That was the question answered on the night of October 17 in game 7.

The Orioles took the lead in the bottom of the 3rd inning when Rich Dauer tagged Pirates starter Jim Bibby for a solo home run. Stargell, who had singled in the 2nd inning, doubled in the 4th. But he was stranded again as Orioles lefthander Scott McGregor pitched himself out of trouble.

The Pirates, however, had been a comeback team all year, and they had confidence in their ability to win the game. Left fielder Bill Robinson rekindled the Pirates' hopes with a one-out single in the top of the 6th inning. That brought Pittsburgh's big number 8, Willie Stargell, to bat. As Stargell headed out of the dugout, a teammate yelled to him, "Come on, Pops, hit one and get us out of here."

Keenly aware of Stargell's great ability to hit a fastball, McGregor started Willie off with a breaking ball. The pitch was just what Stargell, a notorious guess hitter, was looking for. He swung hard and walloped a high drive that headed toward the right-field fence.

Orioles right fielder Ken Singleton raced back to the fence and made a mighty leap, but he could not keep the ball in the park. It dropped beyond his outstretched glove and into the Pirates' bullpen for a home run—Stargell's third of the World Series. Now the Pirates had a 2–1 lead, and that was enough for pitchers Grant Jackson and Kent Tekulve. They made certain that Baltimore never caught up, pitching four hitless innings in relief.

All told, Stargell went 4-for-5 in the seventh game, which gave him a .400 average for the Series. In addition to hitting 3 home runs, he blasted 4 doubles for a total of 7 extra-base hits, a new World Series record. He also collected 7 RBIs, and his 25 total bases tied another Series standard.

It was one of the greatest individual performances in World Series history, and Stargell was unanimously named the Series MVP. When his selection was announced in the Pirates' locker room, Stargell responded with characteristic modesty. "I know only one person can receive the award," he told reporters, "but if I could I would divide it among the entire organization."

Ballplayers often say such things to bolster their own image. But no one doubted Stargell's sincerity. For Willie Stargell, among the game's most feared hitters, was also one of its true gentlemen.

2

SETTING HIS SIGHTS

Wilver Dornell Stargell was born to William and Gladys Stargell on March 6, 1941, just outside of Earlsboro, Oklahoma. Despite his unusual first name — a combination of his father's first name and his mother's middle name, Vernell—he became known to the world as Willie.

Just before Willie was born, William Stargell left Gladys for good. In response, Willie's grandfather, Wil Stargell, took Gladys into his own home and helped her raise Willie. Because of Wil Stargell's devotion to his daughter-in-law and grandson, the Stargell household was a happy one. It was from his grandfather that Willie learned to prize the ideal of family togetherness.

When Willie was about four years old, he and his mother moved to a public housing project in Alameda, California, where she later remarried. Even before he knew what baseball was, Stargell

Willie Stargell (top row, 4th from left) with his high school team in 1958. In 1969, Tommie Harper (top row, 5th from left) stole 76 bases, the most in the A.L. since Ty Cobb stole 96 in 1915. Carl Motton (kneeling, 2nd from right) hit 2 consecutive pinch-hit home runs for Baltimore in 1968.

started "hitting"—he tossed rocks into the air and clubbed them with sticks. Like all great batsmen, he enjoyed the sensation of striking an object solidly and watching it fly into the distance.

As Willie grew older, he joined the neighborhood games of baseball and all its varieties—stickball, whiffle ball, softball, home-run derby—whenever he could. When he had no one else to play with, Stargell tried to hit bottle caps with a broomstick. In doing so, he tried to copy the batting style of N.L. batting champ Stan Musial.

The drives off Stargell's bat kept going farther and farther, and they soon began to break his neighbors' windows. Gladys never asked her son to stop playing ball, but she could not help wondering if his dream of playing major league baseball was anything more than a fantasy.

"Boy, what are you going to do for a living?" she would ask.

"Play ball," Willie always answered.

It was as a member of a youth team representing the public housing projects in which he lived that Stargell got his first taste of intense competition. Around this time, he also began to develop a reputation as a long-ball hitter. He used a cross-handed batting grip. Batting left-handed, he put his right hand on top of his left as if he were a right-handed batter. He refused to change his grip until a friend told him that Hank Aaron had once hit cross-handed but had switched to the more common grip when he realized that it was more effective.

In 1954, Stargell entered Encinal High School, where the boys of the neighboring projects played together on the same teams. Participating in

Stargell in his 1958 high school year book.

basketball, track, football, and baseball, Willie won eight varsity letters. His football career came to an early end when he was tackled from behind and suffered the first of many knee injuries. As a result, he concentrated on his first love, baseball, pointing himself toward a big senior year on the diamond.

George Reed, a recent college graduate, was coach of the Encinal baseball team that year. Coach Reed did not know it, but he had three future major leaguers on his squad: Curt Motton, Tommy Harper, and Willie Stargell. Motton later became a reserve outfielder and valuable pinch-hitter, mostly for Earl Weaver's Baltimore Orioles; Harper played on several American League teams and made the A.L. All-Star lineup in 1970 for the Milwaukee Brewers.

Despite their lack of pitching, the Encinal High baseball team won every game until the league championship in the last game of the

1958 season. Motton and Harper attracted lots of attention from major-league baseball scouts. But Stargell attracted almost none. The Phillies and Yankees expressed a little interest in Willie, but they did not try to sign him.

Finally, Coach Reed begged Pirates scout Bob Zuk to take a good look at Stargell. The first-year scout was not impressed the initial two times he watched Stargell play. The third time, in 1958, Zuk saw something he liked in the lanky, uncoordinated youngster and decided to sign him to a Pittsburgh Pirates contract.

Zuk gambled that when Stargell grew to his full height, he would become a great player. The Pirates scout offered Willie a $1,000 bonus, but Willie's stepfather, Percy Russell, negotiated an additional $500. Stargell's contract also stated that he did not have to report to the minors until the following spring. Zuk knew Stargell was not yet ready for professional baseball and needed to play another summer of amateur ball before

Playing first base during his senior year in high school, Stargell makes the long stretch.

beginning his minor-league career.

Stargell did not enjoy his first year of pro ball in 1959. He was assigned to play in the lowest rung of the minors: the Roswell, New Mexico, club of the Class D Sophomore League. At the ballpark, Stargell and the other black players were often targets for racist fans. Away from the ballpark, blacks were barred from eating in restaurants and staying at motels patronized by their white teammates. Such treatment was extremely difficult for the 18-year-old Stargell to understand. He had never really experienced this kind of racial discrimination before, and he was shocked that people who did not know him could hate him simply for the color of his skin. There were times when he cried himself to sleep. More than once, he called home to tell his mother and stepfather he was thinking of quitting baseball. But even as they sympathized with him, they also told him to stick it out for as long as he could.

Encouraged by his parents and by the Pirates scout who had signed him, Stargell stuck it out in Roswell. He kept his hurt feelings to himself, just as he did a nagging pain in his hip, because he had his sights set on making the big leagues. He was determined not to give anybody the slightest reason to doubt his ability.

3

MOVING UP

In 1959, Willie Stargell was walking through Plainview, Texas, on his way to the ballpark when a man stepped out of an alley and held a shotgun to his head. The man said, "If you play in that game tonight, I'll blow your brains out." Stargell did not know what to do. Name-calling was one thing, but this was something else entirely. "Was baseball worth the risk of being murdered?" he wondered. After hours of agonizing reflection, he decided that baseball was worth the risk.

Stargell did more that just play that night; he played exceedingly well. And after that game, he was more determined than ever to succeed. Whenever obstacles arose, he had only to think of the Plainview incident to know that he could overcome them.

Although his Roswell team finished last in 1959, Stargell had a good season, hitting .274 with 7 home runs and 87 RBIs.

Stargell (2nd from right) at spring training in Daytona Beach, Florida, in 1961. He is wearing the uniform of the Columbus Jets, the Pirates' top minor league team, but he wound up playing for Asheville, a Class A team, that year.

The next year, Stargell moved up to the Class C Northern League. Playing for Grand Forks, North Dakota, he encountered considerably less racial prejudice and was thus able to concentrate more fully on baseball. In his previous year of pro ball, Stargell had hit a lot to the opposite field. But now, as he started adding weight and strength, he began to hit the ball more to center and right fields. While his average dropped to .260, his home run total rose to 11 in 1960.

Stargell also struck out often, but that did not worry him. The Pirates were not worried either. They knew that if Stargell was going to develop his slugging ability to its fullest, he would have to be allowed to swing at the ball with all his might without worrying about striking out. (Among his many major league batting achievements, Stargell would set the N.L. record for most career strikeouts, 1,936.)

On defense, Stargell traded his first baseman's mitt for an outfielder's glove. Pirates manager Danny Murtaugh was hoping that Stargell would one day replace veteran center fielder Bill Virdon. By the end of the 1960 season, Willie had

The starting lineup of the 1961 Asheville Tourists had 4 future major leaguers: (from left to right) Gene Alley (2nd), Jesus McFarlane (4th), Stargell (5th), and Rex Johnson (8th). Stargell hit 22 homers that year, but Gary Rushing (6th from left) was the leader with 25.

become a competent professional outfielder.

While his own team fared poorly again, Stargell avidly followed the exploits of right fielder Roberto Clemente, second baseman Bill Mazeroski, and shortstop Dick Groat as they led the 1960 Pirates to a string of come-from-behind victories and Pittsburgh's first pennant since 1927. When the 1960 Pirates went on to defeat the heavily favored New York Yankees in an exciting seven-game World Series, Stargell felt proud to be part of the organization.

In 1961, Stargell was promoted to the Asheville, North Carolina, team in the Class A Sally League. Asheville was a segregated city, but it had a large black population and Stargell felt very much at home there. Showing more and more power, he learned how to pull the ball and hit .289, collected 89 RBIs, and doubled his home run output to 22. In fact, he hit so many of his homers onto the hill beyond the right-field fence of the Asheville ballpark that the fans began calling him On the Hill Will.

(Years later, after Stargell had established himself in Pittsburgh, he opened a chain of

chicken restaurants, including one in a poor section of town called the Hill District. To promote his restaurants, Stargell gave away free chicken to everyone who was having their order filled when he hit a home run. Pirates broadcaster Bob Prince often encouraged Stargell at bat by saying, "Spread some chicken on the Hill, Will.")

Near the end of the 1961 season, Pirates general manager Joe Brown visited Stargell to congratulate him on his fine showing and to inform him that the Pirates now considered him a genuine prospect for the major leagues.

Asheville won the league title, but Stargell did not rest on his accomplishments. He continued to work on his game, playing winter ball in the Pittsburgh Instructional League team in Arizona. Then, in the spring of 1962, he married his high-school sweetheart, Lois Beard, before reporting to the Pirates' Triple A farm team in Columbus, Ohio.

Stargell really blossomed against the tough competition of the International League. He slugged 27 home runs and hit .276 with 82 RBIs for the Columbus Jets. In mid-September, the Pirates decided to see what he could do against major league pitching and called him up to the big show.

Stargell was immediately impressed by the city of Pittsburgh; its hard-working, sports-loving people; and the Pirates' old ballpark, Forbes Field, which had been built in 1909. The stadium had been home to such Pirates greats as Honus Wagner, Pie Traynor, the Waner brothers, and Ralph Kiner. Stargell was thrilled to be taking batting practice and shagging flies there, and that was all he did for about a week.

Finally, manager Murtaugh sent him in to pinch-hit against Stu Miller, the San Francisco Giants' crafty junkballer. As Stargell went up to bat, the Pirates' veteran first baseman Dick Stuart said, "When you strike out, Rookie, don't feel bad." Miller promptly struck Stargell out with a changeup. But on September 21, he rebounded with the first hit of his major-league career, a triple against the Cincinnati Reds.

Altogether, Stargell got into 10 games and hit .290 during his late-season trial. It was a pretty good debut, and he was well on his way to breaking into the everyday lineup of the Pittsburgh Pirates.

"YOU SHOULD BE PROUD"

Over the winter, the slender Stargell finally filled out; in fact, he became somewhat overweight. The Pirates were very surprised and not at all pleased when he reported to spring training at 235 pounds. As it turned out, the once-skinny Stargell would have to battle to keep his weight down for the rest of his career.

Stargell made the 1963 team, but his official rookie season was not a great one, either for him or for the Pirates. After Pittsburgh dropped to a disappointing seventh-place finish in 1961 and fourth place in 1962, general manager Joe Brown realized that the team would not regain its championship form of 1960 unless some changes were made. That November, Brown traded three-quarters of the Pirates' veteran infield—first baseman Dick Stuart, shortstop Dick Groat, and third baseman Don Hoak—to make room for youngsters Donn Clendenon, Ducky Schofield, and Bob Bailey. When veteran Bob Skinner was

The "Terror Trio" of the Pittsburgh Pirates: (left to right) Stargell, Matty Alou, and Roberto Clemente. Clemente (.328) and Alou (.312) were the major leagues' two top hitters during the 1960s.

Stargell slides neatly around the tag of Mets' catcher Jim Schaffer during a game in 1965. Stargell, never noted for his speed, stole just 17 bases in 33 attempts during his career.

traded to the Cincinnati Reds on May 23, 1963, Stargell was given a shot at the left-field job.

As it turned out, so much inexperience doomed the Pirates, who finished behind everyone but the two 1962 N.L. expansion teams, the Houston Colt 45's and the New York Mets. Stargell belted 11 homers and drove in 47 runs, but he barely hit his weight at .243. The only Pirate batter to have an outstanding year was Roberto Clemente, whose .320 average placed him second in the league.

Already well on his way to a Hall of Fame career, Clemente was the Pirates' undisputed leader. Clemente went out of his way to make rookies, such as Stargell, feel like they were part of the team. "There are only a few hundred major leaguers in the whole world," he told Stargell, "and you should be proud to be one of them." Stargell was truly inspired by Clemente, and the two men became the best of friends. What's more, by watching Clemente, Stargell learned what it took to become a team leader.

Stargell played well enough to establish himself as a regular in 1964, but thumb and knee injuries plus a tooth extraction limited him to 117 games. Nevertheless, his 21 home runs led the Pirates, and he finished second on the team in RBIs with 78. Stargell also made the All-Star team for the first time, though he bounced out in his only at-bat. He had a much better day on July 22, when he knocked out a single, double, triple, and home run to become only the 14th Pirate ever to hit for the cycle. Clendenon, Bailey, Mazeroski, Clemente (who won his second batting title), and pitchers Bob Veale and Al McBean all did well, but the Pirates still had too many weaknesses as a team and finished seventh.

After the season, Stargell underwent surgery to repair his damaged knee. Unfortunately, his marriage was deteriorating, and that was not so easily fixed. Stargell returned to Oakland, where he and Lois, who had borne two daughters, Wendy and Precious, were divorced.

Health problems caused the popular Danny Murtaugh to resign as manager, and in 1965 a new man was put in charge of the Pirates: former N.L. batting champ Harry ("The Hat") Walker. Because Walker did not think Stargell could hit left-handed pitchers, he was platooned in left field. But he had a very good year at the plate. He batted .272, leading the team in home runs and RBIs.

Stargell's hottest hitting came in June —10 home runs and 35 RBIs earned him the N.L.

Player of the Month Award. It was well deserved. On June 8, he hit a mammoth home run over the left-field scoreboard in Forbes Field, the first ever by a left-handed batter. Then on June 24, he hit three home runs in Dodger Stadium, barely missing a fourth, which wound up as a double.

Stargell made the N.L. All-Star team again, and this time he was named to the starting lineup. "This is some kind of thrill," said Stargell. "I still can't believe it." Stargell's first-inning single off Milt Pappas and his second-inning homer off Jim ("Mudcat") Grant helped the National League to its 6–5 victory over the American Leaguers. Strangely, Stargell's heroics in the game were his last in All-Star competition. Although he played in five more All-Star contests, he did not hit safely in any of them.

As for the Pirates, they improved dramatically under Walker in 1965. Their 90–72 record boosted them all the way to third place behind the Dodgers and Giants. The 1966 season was almost an instant replay of 1965, with the Dodgers, behind the pitching of Sandy Koufax and Don Drysdale, winning their second pennant in a row. The Pirates finished third again.

Stargell came into his own that year, as he slugged 33 home runs and knocked in 102 runs while hitting .315, the highest season's average he would ever compile. He also racked up 9 straight hits in two games against the Houston Astros on June 4 and 5. For the second year in a row, he was named the left fielder on *The Sporting News*'s post-season N.L. All-Star team.

By this time, Stargell had made Pittsburgh his year-round home. Thankful for his good fortune, he began working with the city's poor and underprivileged. On November 19, he mar-

Dolores Stargell looks on during spring training in 1970, while three-year-old Willie Stargell, Jr., climbs the fence to get a better look at his dad.

ried a local model, Dolores Parker, who later gave birth to a son, Wilver, Jr., and daughter, Kelli Lorraine. Unfortunately, Stargell sampled too much of his wife's fine cooking over the winter of 1966–67, and his extra weight contributed to a slow start in the spring.

Excited about the team's improvement and a trade that brought Maury Wills, the Dodgers' base-stealing king, to the club, Pittsburgh fans had first-place expectations in 1967. But the team played sluggishly and dropped to fifth place with a disappointing 81–81 record. Plagued by nagging minor injuries and management's focus on his weight problem, Stargell saw his average fall to .271 with 20 home runs and 73 RBIs.

In another off-season trade, the Pirates acquired strikeout artist Jim Bunning to strengthen their pitching staff for 1968, and once again Pittsburgh fans were dreaming of a pennant. The team played inconsistently under new manager Larry Shepard, however, and finished far out of the money at 80–82. Stargell started off slowly but went on a hot streak after a three-homer game on May 22 against the Cubs in Wrigley Field. As luck would have it, two painful collisions with outfield walls slowed Stargell down, and he finished the year at .237. Even so, his 24 homers were tops on the team.

Stargell bounced back to have a fine all-around year in 1969, batting .307 with 29 home runs and 92 RBIs. One of those homers, off Alan

On July 16 1970, the Pirates left Forbes Field for Three Rivers Stadium. The Pirates lost to the Reds, 3–2, in the inaugural game at the new park, but Stargell hit the first home run there by a Pirate.

Foster, soared completely out of Dodger Stadium—the first ever to do so —and traveled 506 feet. Dodger pitcher Don Sutton said, "I'm glad it wasn't me. Stargell doesn't just hit pitchers. He takes away their dignity."

Playing in the newly formed six-team Eastern Division of the National League, the Pirates improved to 88–74 in 1969 but still came in third behind the "Miracle" Mets, who went on to surprise victories in both the first N.L. championship series and the World Series.

Now an established star and already the Pirates' all-time leading left-handed home-run hitter, Stargell yearned more than ever to play on a championship Pittsburgh team. His deepest desire would soon be fulfilled as he and the team entered a new, exciting era in Pirates history.

THE HOME RUN KING

Willie Stargell was not unduly worried when he began the 1970 season in an 0-for-23 slump. He knew he would eventually start hitting, and so did Danny Murtaugh, back on the job as the Bucs' manager. The confidence that Murtaugh showed in Stargell and the other Pirates was a big factor in the team's success that year.

Though struggling at the plate, Stargell finally hit two long home runs onto the right-field roof of Forbes Field in the last week of April. These two shots increased his total to 7 of the 18 balls that were hit onto or over the right-field roof in the long history of Forbes Field, which was quickly coming to an end. Built in four months for $2 million, Forbes Field would soon be replaced by Three Rivers Stadium, a modern multipurpose arena with synthetic turf that the city of Pittsburgh had been building for two years at a cost of $55 million. On the verge of finally putting it all together, the Pirates were eager to begin a new winning tradition in their new ballpark.

On June 12, Stargell's long-ball hitting helped Dock Ellis win a no-hitter against San Diego, 2–0. Stargell hit two home runs in the game.

The Pirates were a first-place team when they opened Three Rivers Stadium on July 16, 1970. Their new double-knit uniforms, the first ever worn in the major leagues, also made them the best-dressed team in baseball. Appropriately, they faced the Western Division leaders, the Cincinnati Reds, who would become the Pirates' post-season rivals for much of the 1970s. The Reds spoiled the opening of Three Rivers by winning the game 3–2, but Stargell won a $1,000 bonus by hitting the first Pirates homer in the new stadium.

Pumped up by the team's new home and their sleek new uniforms, Stargell mounted a strong comeback in the second half of the season. On August 1 against Atlanta, he tied a major-league record by ringing up five extra-base hits (two homers and three doubles) in one game, and eight days later he hit his first upper-deck home run at Three Rivers, off the Mets' Ron Taylor. (Willie Stargell would knock two more balls into the upper decks at Three Rivers in 1971 and a fourth in 1973.)

By the end of the 1970 season, Stargell had his average up to a respectable .264, and his 85 RBIs and 31 home runs led the team. Of far more importance to him than his own statistics was the fact that Pittsburgh had clinched the Eastern Division title on September 21.

Stargell and the Pirates were now one step away from a World Series berth. One big step, as it turned out. Though all three games were close, the Reds swept the Pirates in the N.L. playoffs. The Pirates' lack of hitting was their downfall, as only third baseman Richie Hebner (4-for-6) and Stargell (6-for-12) hit well.

That winter, Stargell and four other major-

league players flew to Vietnam to visit hospitalized U.S. servicemen. Deeply touched by the courage and self-sacrifice of the injured soldiers, Stargell found himself wanting to do something more to help his fellow man. Because his daughter Wendy suffered from sickle-cell anemia, Stargell decided to organize an annual bowling tournament to raise funds toward the cure of the disease. A decade later, he would receive an honorary Doctor of Humanities degree from St. Francis College in Loretto, Pennsylvania, for his contributions to sickle-cell anemia research.

Armed with a new perspective on life and rededicated to helping the Pirates become the best team in baseball, Stargell produced the greatest season of his career in 1971. He slammed 9 home runs in the Pirates' first 15 games and a record 11 homers in the month of

Stargell singles in game 2 of the 1971 World Series. Facing the Orioles' four 20-game winners, the victorious Pirates scored just 23 runs in 7 games.

April. Included in this barrage were two other three-homer games, on April 10 and April 21. Nobody in baseball history, not even Babe Ruth or Roger Maris, had ever hit so many homers that early in the season. By the time the All-Star break came around, Stargell had hit 30 home runs and had 87 RBIs, and he wound up with a league-leading 48 homers and 125 RBIs. There is no telling what kind of totals he would have compiled if another knee injury had not slowed him down late in the season.

Understandably, Stargell was disappointed when he finished second to the Cardinals' Joe Torre in the voting for the league MVP Award, especially because it was his big bat that drove the Pirates to another Eastern Division championship.

As much as they valued Stargell's contribution, the Pirates were hardly a one-man team.

Stargell and Clemente, the two leaders of the Pirates, hug Al Oliver after his three-run homer against the Giants in the N.L. playoffs gave the Pirates the 1971 N.L. pennant.

They proved this by knocking off the San Francisco Giants 3-games-to-1 in the N.L. playoffs, even though Stargell went 0-for-14. First baseman Bob Robertson took up the slack, blasting three home runs for Pittsburgh in game 2 and a fourth in game 3.

Stargell did a little better in the World Series against the powerful Baltimore Orioles, getting 5 hits in 24 at-bats, but again it was a teammate who wore the hero's laurels. With outstanding defense and a Series-leading 12 hits (including 5 for extra bases), Roberto Clemente led the Pirates to a thrilling come-from-behind victory after Pittsburgh had lost the first two games in Baltimore. Baltimore manager Earl Weaver said afterward, "Roberto Clemente almost single-handedly beat my team." Despite his lackluster work at bat, Stargell was proud to score what turned out to be the winning run in the 8th inning of the crucial seventh game.

During the off-season, Stargell had surgery on his left knee. And when Robertson slumped badly in early 1972, Stargell wound up playing more first base than left field for the first time in his major league career. Although the move to first greatly reduced the wear and tear on his knees, Stargell was not a great first baseman. In fact, he led the league's first sackers in errors, and the following year he returned to left field.

Stargell's numbers were down in 1972 from the previous year. But his 33 homers, 112 RBIs, and .293 average still made for a terrific season. Under new manager Bill Virdon, the Pirates continued to perform like a dynasty in the making, especially on offense. A record nine Pittsburgh hitters collected 100 or more hits over the season: Stargell, second baseman Dave Cash,

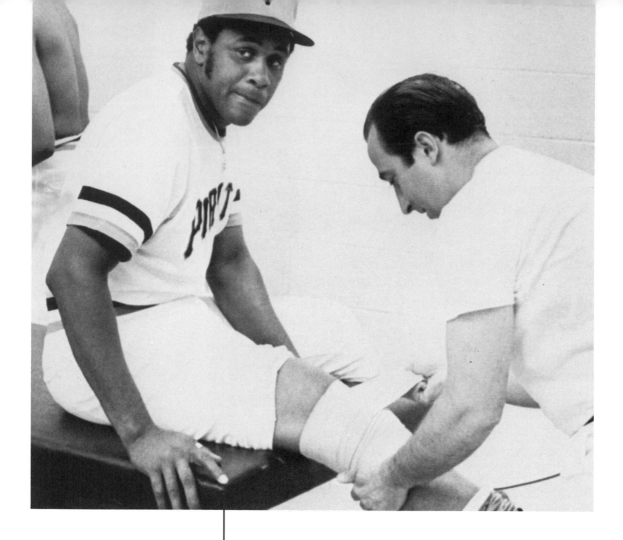

Trainer Tony Bartirome, a former Pirates player, tapes Stargell's knee. Plagued with knee problems that slowed him in the outfield, Willie began playing mostly at first base after the 1971 season.

Hebner, left fielder Vic Davalillo, center fielder Al Oliver, Clemente, catcher Manny Sanguillen, reserve outfielder Gene Clines, and utility man Rennie Stennett. Not surprisingly, the Pirates won their third Eastern Division title in a row with a 96–59 record and enjoyed an 11-game lead over the second-place Chicago Cubs.

The N.L. championship playoffs opened in Pittsburgh and again pitted the Pirates against the Cincinnati Reds. Stargell's RBI double was part of a three-run first inning that led the Pirates to a 5–1 win in the opener. The Reds got even the next day, however, with a four-run first inning paving the way for a 5-3 victory. The two teams also split games 3 and 4, but the Reds won the exciting clincher, 4–3, with two clutch runs in the bottom of the 9th.

The season ended on a disappointing note. But the loss of a championship was nothing compared to the loss Stargell and his teammates would soon suffer.

6

THE BIGGEST LOSS

Young Todd Shubin talks to Stargell after he hit a ball out of Dodgers Stadium on May 8, 1973, and Shubin retrieved the ball in the parking lot. Stargell is the only man to hit a home run completely out of Dodger Stadium, and he did it twice, the first time in 1969.

On New Year's Eve, 1972, an old four-engine propeller airplane took off from the San Juan, Puerto Rico, airport. The purpose of the flight was to bring aid to the survivors of an earthquake that had recently devastated the city of Managua, Nicaragua. Overloaded with food and supplies, the plane experienced engine trouble as it lifted off, and it crashed into the Atlantic Ocean about a mile from shore. All five persons aboard died in the crash, including Roberto Clemente, who was leading the mission of mercy.

The death of Clemente shocked and saddened the entire baseball world, and Willie Stargell, like most of Clemente's teammates, cried when he heard the terrible news. Clemente received many posthumous honors, including immediate election into the Baseball Hall of Fame in March. In his memory, circular patches with his number, 21, were sewn onto the left sleeves of all the Pirates' jerseys.

For years, Clemente had been the acknowledged leader of the Pittsburgh Pirates. Now that he was gone. Stargell's quiet leadership qualities were needed more than ever, and in the spring of 1973 he was named official captain of the team.

The Pirates did a good job of replacing Clemente in right field. Initially, catcher Manny Sanguillen, Clemente's closest friend on the team, played right with reserve Milt May taking over behind the plate. However, Sanguillen eventually went back to catching and right field was turned over to rookie Richie Zisk, who came through like a veteran, hitting .325 with 10 homers and 54 RBIs.

Replacing Clemente's indomitable spirit was a lot more difficult, and the Pirates stumbled their way through the 1973 season. Trying to lead the team by example, Stargell produced one of the most outstanding years of his career. He batted .299 while leading the league in doubles (43), home runs (44), slugging percentage (.646), and RBIs (119). Stargell's 302nd home run on July 11 made him the Pirates' all-time home run leader. The three triples he hit that year (along with his 43 doubles and 44 homers) gave him a grand total of 90 extra-base hits for the 1973 season, another Pirates record.

But Stargell's great example was not enough. Even with the entire division playing poorly, the Bucs could not take command of the East. In early September, Danny Murtaugh came back as manager, replacing Bill Virdon, but the switch did not help. Pittsburgh finished third with an 80–82 record. The New York Mets came in first with the worst record (82–79) ever for a divisional champion. In a controversial vote, Pete Rose beat out Stargell in the voting for the league's MVP Award. Rose had a fine year, winning his third batting title, but critics said that it was no better than several other seasons he had had, and that the writers had decided to, in effect, honor the whole Reds' team by giving Rose the award.

The next year presented another problem for Pittsburgh. Even as the Pirates were recovering from the loss of Clemente, they had to adjust to a bunch of new young faces in the lineup. Rennie Stennett replaced Dave Cash at second base; Frank Taveras moved in as the regular short-stop; and big Dave Parker made the team as a backup outfielder. Stargell, by now one of the team's veteran players, took a special interest in the talented Parker, who soon blossomed into one of the league's superstars.

Habitually slow starters, the Pirates came out crawling in 1974. They lost their first 6 games and 10 of their first 12. Mired in last place for the season's first 10 weeks, they clearly

A grief-stricken Stargell and his wife leave the funeral services for Roberto Clemente, who died in a plane crash on New Year's Eve, 1972.

Stargell's 1966 Topps bubble gum card.

needed a spark of some kind to get them going. It came on July 14 in the second game of a doubleheader against the Cincinnati Reds, when both teams engaged in a bench-clearing brawl after trading knockdown pitches.

Nobody was seriously hurt, but the fight lit a competitive fire in the Pirates, who beat the Reds, 2–1. The win ended a five-game Pirates losing streak and started an eight-game winning streak that thrust the team into contention. With solid efforts from pitchers Jim Rooker, Jerry Reuss, Ken Brett, and Dock Ellis and some excellent offense from Richie Zisk, Al Oliver, and Stargell, Pittsburgh moved into first place on August 25 by sweeping a doubleheader from the San Diego Padres. The Pirates battled gamely to stay there and clinched the divisional title on the last day of the season. It was their fourth N.L. East title in the last five years. They now faced the winners in the West, the Los Angeles Dodgers.

In winning 102 games during the regular season, the Dodgers also led the league in homers and runs scored. L.A.'s pitching was especially strong, boasting a 20-game winner (Andy Messersmith), a 19-game winner (Don Sutton), and the N.L. Cy Young Award winner, reliever Mike Marshall, who had appeared in a record 106 games.

Although the Dodger pitchers had the league's lowest ERA, Pittsburgh won game 3, 7–0, with Stargell and Hebner each driving in three runs; but in the other three playoff contests, the Dodger aces held the Pirates to 3 measly runs while Dodger hitters put 20 runs on the scoreboard. Stargell's 7th-inning homer accounted for Pittsburgh's lone tally in a lopsided

12–1 Los Angeles victory in the finale.

In 1975, Stargell moved back to the infield as the Pirates' regular first baseman. His fielding improved, and first base remained his position for the rest of his career. At 34 years of age, Stargell was now slowing down. He missed 18 games due to a cracked rib and batted 461 times in 1975, his lowest total since 1968. He also failed for the first time since 1967 to lead the Pirates in home runs. That honor went to his protégé, Dave Parker, who hit 25 homers and also led the team in RBIs with 101. Nevertheless, Stargell's .295 average, 22 homers, and 90 RBIs proved that his bat was still potent.

The Pirates continued to dominate in the East, winning their fifth divisional crown of the decade. The Pirates entered the playoffs hoping that their third try against the Cincinnati Reds in the 1970s would do the trick.

The only problem was that this Reds team was even better than the Cincinnati teams that had defeated the Pirates in 1970 and 1972. The Big Red Machine, powered by Johnny Bench, Tony Perez, Joe Morgan, and Pete Rose, would go on to win back-to-back World Series. And they took their first step on the road to glory by handily sweeping the Pirates for the N.L. pennant.

It was another painful setback, but the Pirates were not about to become discouraged. For their clubhouse leader, Willie Stargell, had taught them how to face adversity. "If you win like men, you got to lose like men," he said. Unfortunately, Stargell would be forced to take his own advice in 1976, when he experienced what he described as the "most trying year of my life."

CHANGING TIMES

The Pirates opened the 1976 season with a menacing lineup of fence-busters, known as the Lumber Company: Rennie Stennett, Richie Hebner, Al Oliver, Dave Parker, Richie Zisk, Manny Sanguillen, and Willie Stargell. The team got off to a fast start. Then an off-the-field crisis brought Stargell's season to a terrifying halt.

On the evening of May 24, Stargell and his wife, Dolores, were at home watching television when she began suffering an excruciating headache. Several aspirins did not make her feel any better. In fact, she began vomiting. Stargell rushed her to the hospital, but the doctors could find nothing wrong. As the Stargells were leaving the hospital, however, Dolores had a seizure, so Stargell rushed her back into the emergency room. This time, the doctors discovered that

Stargell breaks his bat hitting a double against the Phillies on September 23, 1975. The two-bagger drove in a run and clinched the pennant for the Bucs. Observing how hard it was to hit, Stargell said, "They give you a round bat and they throw you a round ball. And they tell you to hit it square."

Dolores had a blood clot in the lower part of her brain.

Dolores's condition quickly worsened, and the doctors had to operate immediately to save her life. The delicate surgery, which took 2½ hours, was successful, but Dolores remained in critical condition for days while Stargell maintained a vigil at her bedside.

Stargell's reaction to the crisis was typical of him. "I couldn't let myself hit rock-bottom," he explained. "That's the easy way out. Throw up your hands and quit. That's not what my life has been. That's not what it's going to be." Instead, Stargell became a source of strength for his children, constantly assuring them that everything would be okay, and the family drew closer together than ever.

Dolores slowly made a complete recovery, but Stargell's concentration on the diamond was severely affected and he had a subpar season. He managed to hit 20 home runs in 1976 —the 13th year in a row he had hit at least that many—but his average dropped to .257 and his RBI total to 65.

As for the other Pirates, they were having troubles of their own—and from a totally unexpected source. The traditionally woeful Philadelphia Phillies had gained dramatically on the Pirates in 1975, finishing second just behind them. And in 1976, they passed right by the Bucs to take the East by a comfortable nine-game margin. The Pirates' 92–70 record was good only for second place.

Danny Murtaugh retired after the 1976 season, so Pittsburgh had a new manager for 1977, Chuck Tanner. He had been the manager of the Oakland A's in 1976 and came to Pittsburgh in

Stargell received a Doctor of Humanities degree from St. Francis College for his work with the Stargell Foundation to find a cure for sickle-cell anemia. He ended his acceptance speech by saying, "I guess this means I'm a doctor now. Does anyone want to volunteer for surgery?"

a trade for catcher Manny Sanguillen. He immediately began making changes. Familiar with American League players, Tanner sent Richie Zisk to the Chicago White Sox for two hard-throwing young relievers, Rich ("Goose") Gossage and Terry Forster. He obtained veteran Phil Garner from Oakland to replace third baseman Hebner, who had signed with the Phillies as a free agent. And he made slender Omar Moreno, one of the fastest men in baseball, his regular center fielder.

Tanner wanted to bat Frank Taveras first and Moreno second in order to give the Pirates' lineup some much-needed base-stealing capability at the top of the order. He also dropped Stargell, who had always been the club's cleanup hitter, to fifth. Stargell accepted the situation graciously, and Tanner, who could have been put on the spot, was greatly impressed with the veteran's unselfishness. "It was a big thing on his part to move from fourth to fifth, and I knew right there what kind of leader he was," said Tanner. "His attitude in the clubhouse inspires everyone. What a great honor it is for me to manage a player like Willie Stargell."

Adopting Tanner's aggressive style of play, the Pirates battled the Phillies for the divisional lead from the very beginning of the 1977 season. Stargell was hampered in April by an inner-ear ailment that caused him headaches and dizzy spells; but he got hot in the first week of May, batting .455 (10-for-22) with 5 home runs and 10 RBIs to earn N.L. Player of the Week honors.

On June 29, Stargell reached a milestone in his career when he connected off St. Louis Cardinals pitcher Eric Rasmussen to become the first Pirate ever to hit 400 home runs. Stargell hit only one more homer all season, however, because of an elbow injury he suffered on July 9 while trying to break up a brush-back free-for-all, this time involving the Phillies. Stargell tried to keep playing, but on August 5 he was put on the disabled list for the remainder of the season. He eventually needed surgery to relocate the ulnar nerve in his left elbow to its proper place.

The Pirates stayed in the race a long time, winning 96 games. But they eventually took a back seat to the Phillies, who repeated as Eastern Division champs on the strength of a 101–61 record.

The so-called experts looked at Stargell's statistics for 1977, his 13 homers and 35 RBIs, and concluded that he was all washed up. They did not seem to notice that Stargell had played in only 63 games; they focused simply on the fact that his home run and RBI totals were the lowest since his rookie year.

Obviously, these observers did not know Willie Stargell very well. He had learned long ago to listen to his heart, not to the doubts of others. He was not about to let anyone tell him it was time to retire when he still got a thrill putting on his Pirates uniform. On the other hand, Stargell knew that baseball was a demanding game. "If you take it for granted, it will embarrass you," he said. So he worked hard all winter to prepare for the next season.

The 1978 Pirates finished second behind the Phillies for the third year in a row, but the 36-year-old Stargell had a terrific season. In only 390 at-bats, he averaged .295 with 28 home runs and 97 RBIs. He also collected the 2,000th hit of his career on September 3 and the 11th grand slam on September 30, which tied him for the all-time Pirates lead with Ralph Kiner. Nobody was surprised when Stargell was named the N.L. Comeback Player of the Year. The real surprise would come in 1979.

A HAPPY ENDING

After finishing only 1½ games behind the Phillies in 1978, the Pirates considered themselves the team to beat in the East as they headed into 1979.

It did not look that way at first, however. The Pirates got off to yet another bad start, winning just 4 of their first 14 games. Acquiring fiery shortstop Tim Foli from the New York Mets for Frank Taveras helped, but the team was still misfiring by early May. It was then that Stargell called a clubhouse meeting to remind his teammates that a slow start had cost them the previous year's pennant. Stargell's pep talk had the desired effect, and the team began to click.

To reward extra efforts, Stargell bought gold stars that he awarded to his teammates when they played well. The Pirates proudly displayed their stars on their caps. Also at Stargell's instigation, the Pirates adopted the hit record "We Are Family" by Sister Sledge as their theme song. It was not long before the fans had adopted it as well. Three Rivers Stadium would rock when the song was played during a Pirates rally.

Stargell connects for a 2-run homer against the Orioles' Scott McGregor in the 1979 World Series. Stargell hit .400 in the series with 7 extra-base hits.

Stargell himself started well, but he was sidelined for a while by a hip injury. John Milner did a great job filling in for him at first base, and teammates Bill Robinson, Mike Easler, and Dave Parker took turns carrying the team offensively.

By the last week of June, the Pirates were in second place. On June 28, they traded with the Giants for third baseman Bill ("Mad Dog") Madlock, who would be instrumental in their drive toward the pennant, raising his batting average by 20 points, to .328, after coming to the Pirates. As the teams broke for the All-Star Game in July, the Pirates were in fourth place in the N.L. East, but they were just four games behind the leader, the surprising Montreal Expos.

The Pirates and the Montreal Expos tangled throughout September in a red-hot divisional rivalry. After whipping the Expos in Montreal, the Pirates needed to split two games with the Cubs to clinch a tie for the pennant. The Cubs took the first game, and as September 30 dawned, the Pirates were faced with a must-win game. It was Prize Day at Three Rivers Stadium, and the biggest prize was Willie Stargell. He drove in the first run with a sacrifice fly, and the Bucs scored again before Stargell came to bat in the 4th. The Captain hit a long shot over the right field fence to make it 3–0. In the 7th, the Cubs walked Stargell to load the bases, and Robinson drove in two runs with a single. With five runs across, the Pirate family started to rock, the frustrations of the previous three seasons forgotten.

Though Stargell batted just .222 in September, he also cracked 8 home runs, including four game-winners, while driving in 18 runs down the stretch. That gave Stargell a .281 average for the season along with 32 homers, tops for the

In an emotional tribute to
one of Pittsburgh's favorite
stars, the Pirates honored
Stargell on July 20, 1980.
Overcome by the celebration,
a tearful Stargell hugs
his mother.

Pirates, and 82 RBIs. For leading the Pirates to
the Eastern Division title he finally won the N.L.
MVP Award, although he had to share the honor
with St. Louis's Keith Hernandez.

Once again, the Pirates faced the Western
Division champion Reds in the playoffs. Cincinnati had kept Pittsburgh out of the World Series
in 1970, 1972, and 1975, but this year the
Pirates were determined to go all the way.

The first game of the 1979 playoffs went into
extra innings, tied 2–2. In the 11th, against
reliever Tom Hume, Tim Foli and Dave Parker led
off with singles, and then Stargell homered to
right to give Pittsburgh an insurmountable 5–2
lead.

The Pirates, with Stargell singling and dou-
bling in three at-bats, took another extra-inning

affair, 3–2, the next night. Then they headed home to Pittsburgh one victory away from the National League pennant.

With more heavy hitting by Stargell, who contributed a solo homer and a two-run double, the Pirates sailed past the Reds in game 3, 7–1, to complete the sweep. Altogether, Stargell hit .455 with 2 doubles, 2 homers, and 6 RBIs, one more than the Reds collected as a team. Stargell's performance made him an easy choice as the playoffs' MVP.

The confident Pirates then faced the Baltimore Orioles, their opponents in 1971, the last year they were in the World Series. The Orioles stunned the Pirates by striking for five big runs in the bottom of the first inning of the opener. Stargell drove in two runs with a groundout and an 8th-inning home run as the Bucs gamely fought back, but the Orioles held on for a 5–4 victory. The Pirates were happy to leave Baltimore with a split after veteran catcher Manny Sanguillen (acquired back from Oakland in 1979) won game 2 with a 9th-inning pinch-hit RBI single that broke a 2–2 tie.

But when the Pirates returned home to Three Rivers Stadium, disaster struck. The Orioles jumped all over Pittsburgh pitching for 25 hits, 17 runs, and convincing 8–4, 9–6 wins in games 3 and 4 to take a 3-games-to-1 Series lead. Stargell had three hits and another home run by game 4, but it was not enough. It looked as if the Pirates' magic had finally run out.

The Pirates pulled another of their patented comebacks to win the fifth and sixth games, however, and set the stage for Stargell's great performance in the seventh and final game.

Stargell's MVP Award in the World Series

capped his tremendous season and made him the first person ever to be named an MVP of the regular season, a league championship series, and the World Series all in the same year. After 17 years of outstanding work, Stargell was finally recognized as one of baseball's best.

On July 20, 1980, the Pirates held Willie Stargell Day at Three Rivers Stadium. On September 6, 1982, another Willie Stargell Day was held, and this time Pop's uniform number, 8, was retired before the game with the Mets. More than 38,000 fans then roared their approval when Stargell stroked a pinch-hit single in the Pirates' 6–1 win.

Three weeks later, Stargell finally called it quits. In his 2,360-game career, he had batted .282. He retired as the Pirates' all-time leader in home runs, RBIs, and extra-base hits.

Stargell went to work as the Pirates' minor-league batting instructor in 1984, and a year later he was named the Pirates' first-base coach. In 1986, he rejoined his friend Chuck Tanner, who was managing in Atlanta, and coached for the Braves until Tanner was fired midway through the 1988 season.

On July 31, 1988, Stargell stood proudly on the podium at Cooperstown, New York, where he was inducted into the National Baseball Hall of Fame. The 200th member, he was only the 17th to be elected in his first year of eligibility. Stargell spoke with great humility and thankfulness that day and even took time out to deliver a heartfelt message: "To the young people, I'd like to say that I am living proof that hard work brings rewards. There are no shortcuts." It was vintage Stargell. On the biggest day of his life, he was still thinking about helping other people.

CHRONOLOGY

March 6, 1941	Born in Earlsboro, Oklahoma
1958	Signs with Pittoburgh Pirates
Sept. 21, 1962	Gets first major league hit
1964	Makes N.L. All-Star team for first time
June 4–5, 1966	Cracks nine straight hits vs. Astros
Aug. 6, 1969	Becomes first batter to ever hit a fair ball completely out of Dodger Stadium
July 16, 1970	Hits first home run in Pittsburgh's new Three Rivers Stadium
Aug. 1, 1970	Ties a major-league record by getting five extra-base hits (three doubles, two homers) in a game
April 1971	Has two three-home-run games in one month (April 10 and 21); sets record for home runs in April with 11
1973	Named captain of the Pirates
July 11, 1973	Hits home run number 302 to become all-time Pirate leader
1973	Leads N.L. in home runs (44), RBIs (119), and doubles (43)
Sept. 3, 1978	Collects 2,000th hit (a single)
1978	Voted Comeback Player of the Year by *The Sporting News*
1979	Voted Co-MVP of the N.L., MVP of the N.L.C.S., and MVP of the World Series
Sept. 6, 1982	Pirates hold Willie Stargell Day and retire his uniform number, 8
1985	Coaches for the Pittsburgh Pirates
1986–88	Coaches for the Atlanta Braves
Jan. 12, 1988	Elected to the Hall of Fame in his first year of eligibility

WILVER DORNEL STARGELL
"WILLIE"
PITTSBURGH, N.L., 1962 - 1982
INTIMIDATING PRESENCE BETWEEN THE LINES
AND CHARISMATIC PATRIARCH IN CLUBHOUSE
AND DUGOUT. CRUSHED 475 HOMERS, MANY
OF TAPE-MEASURE VARIETY AND HIT MOST
BY ANY PLAYER DURING 1970'S. LIKE HIS
ROUND-TRIPPERS, HIS 1,540 RBI'S ALSO MOST
EVER BY A PIRATE. BATTED .282 OVER 21
SEASONS, ALL WITH PITTSBURGH. SHARED N.L.
MVP HONORS IN 1979, AND NAMED MVP IN '79
N.L. CHAMPIONSHIP SERIES AND WORLD SERIES.

© 1988 NBHOF

MAJOR LEAGUE STATISTICS

PITTSBURGH PIRATES

Year	Team	G	AB	R	H	2B	3B	HR	RBI	BA	SB
1962	PITT N	10	31	1	9	3	1	0	4	.290	0
1963		108	304	34	74	11	6	11	47	.243	0
1964		117	421	53	115	19	7	21	78	.273	1
1965		144	533	68	145	25	8	27	107	.272	1
1966		140	485	84	153	30	0	33	102	.315	2
1967		134	462	54	125	18	6	20	73	.271	1
1968		128	435	57	103	15	1	24	67	.237	5
1969		145	522	89	160	31	6	29	92	.307	1
1970		136	474	70	125	18	3	31	85	.264	0
1971		141	511	104	151	26	0	48	125	.295	0
1972		138	495	75	145	28	2	33	112	.293	1
1973		148	522	106	156	43	3	44	119	.299	0
1974		140	508	90	153	37	4	25	96	.301	0
1975		124	461	71	136	32	2	22	90	.295	0
1976		117	428	54	110	20	3	20	65	.257	2
1977		63	186	29	51	12	0	13	35	.274	0
1978		122	390	60	115	18	2	28	97	.295	3
1979		126	424	60	119	19	0	32	82	.281	0
1980		67	202	28	53	10	1	11	38	.262	0
1981		38	60	2	17	4	0	0	9	.283	0
1982		74	73	6	17	4	0	3	17	.233	0
TOTAL		2360	7927	1195	2232	423	55	475	1540	.282	17

League Championship Series

(6 years)		22	79	8	20	5	0	4	12	.253	0

World Series

(2 years)		14	54	10	17	5	0	3	8	.315	0

All-Star Games

(7 years)		7	10	3	2	0	0	1	2	.200	0

FURTHER READING

Charlton, James. *The Baseball Chronology*. New York: Macmillan, 1991.

Hill, Susan and Bob Adelman. *Out of Left Field: Willie Stargell's Turning Point Season*. New York: Proteus, 1980.

Honig, Donald. *The Power Hitters*. St. Louis: The Sporting News, 1989.

Libby, Bill. *Willie Stargell: Baseball Slugger*. New York: G.P. Putnam, 1973.

Sahadi, Lou. *The Pirates: "We Are Family."* New York: Times Books, 1980.

Shatzkin, Mike, ed. *The Ballplayers*. New York: William Morrow, 1990.

Stargell, Willie and Tom Bird. *Willie Stargell: An Autobiography*. New York: Harper & Row, 1984.

INDEX

MIKE SHANNON is the editor and publisher of *Spitball, the Literary Baseball Magazine* and the author of *Diamond Classics: Essays on 100 of the Best Baseball Books Ever Published*. He has also edited *The Best of Spitball* anthology and written three chapbooks of baseball poetry. Born in Wilmington, North Carolina, and raised in Jacksonville, Florida, he is a graduate of N.C. Wesleyan College and Xavier (OH) University. He lives in Cincinnati, Ohio, with his wife Kathleen Dermody Shannon and their children Meghann, Casey, Mickey, Babe, and Nolan Ryan.

JIM MURRAY, veteran sports columnist of the *Los Angeles Times*, is one of America's most acclaimed writers. He has been named "America's Best Sportswriter" by the National Association of Sportscasters and Sportswriters 14 times, was awarded the Red Smith Award, and was twice winner of the National Headliner Award. In addition, he was awarded the J. G. Taylor Spink Award in 1987 for "meritorious contributions to baseball writing." With this award came his 1988 induction into the National Baseball Hall of Fame in Cooperstown, New York. In 1990, Jim Murray was awarded the Pulitzer Prize for Commentary.

EARL WEAVER is the winningest manager in Baltimore Orioles history by a wide margin. He compiled 1,480 victories in his 17 years at the helm. After managing eight different minor league teams, he was given the chance to lead the Orioles in 1968. Under his leadership the Orioles finished lower than second place in the American League East only four times in 17 years. One of only 12 managers in big league history to have managed in four or more World Series, Earl was named Manager of the Year in 1979. The popular Weaver had his number 4 retired in 1982, joining Brooks Robinson, Frank Robinson, and Jim Palmer, whose numbers were retired previously. Earl Weaver continues his association with the professional baseball scene by writing, broadcasting, and coaching.